Socks my cat and his snakes

Socks my cat.
What are his Toys?
What brings him joy?
A long nap?
Sitting on my, lap?
Jumping the dog? Driving her nuts?
Reminding me of my place?
By putting his Ass in my face?
No, no, no.
Playing with balls of string?
Almost like a human thing?
No, no, no.
Being surrounded by his pride
of ho's?
No, no, no.
He isn't happy unless he's
playing with
garden snakes.
Slapping them around.
Happier than a hound.
Doesn't need a soccer ball, doesn't need a hacky
sack.
but fortunately, for the snake.
its not sock's snack.

Two young squirrels

two young ones in my tree.
they seem to be free.
running around the tree.
Tails high in the air running
around. the noises they make
such a wonderful sound.
Just make sure there's, no,
walnuts around. or fur will
fly.
they only times they stop
 is when cats walk by.

The damn cold.

Making my disabled body hurt.
The wind hitting me like a slap in the face.
Keeping me inside.
Keeping me locked in.
Almost like punishing me for a secrete sin.
Yes, I'm warm, yes I'm home.
But with out caring human touch,
laughter that's not audio or a TV screen.
All this alone time,
feels like a never ending, bad dream.
Curse this cold.
Curse this winter day, that seems, more like
night.
All I see in my sight is that cursed white.
Long for the days of spring.
So once again my heart will be able to sing.
I'm tired of winters slumber.

A Winters scene

he biting wind
sends its blows.
like a flogger does on a slaves back side.
no matter how you turn.
with the wind and flogger,
you feel the coldness
then the burn.
the body becomes warm
with sensations.
The noises, loud and soft.
are beautiful creation

Robin Red Breast

Robin, robin, red breast.
Every spring you come to see me.
You give me hope, you give me, joy.
A sign of spring.
Robin there is a two story green house next to
me.
There on a window seal, you, I do see. Do you
stay there
to keep from being a cats meal? What do you see
in that
empty house? What attracts you?
What keeps you there? A trapped spouse?
Why spend so much time at that empty shell?
You fly there, you sit there, day after day.
I'm a loss for words.
I just don't know what to say.
your persistence, surprises even me.

The Cross I bare

Some see a disability as a bad thing.
How can it be positive? you ask.
Jesus had rougher cross to bare.
He gave himself up for my sin.
His life was spent helping others.
Loving others. Sister, brothers.
Not just family and friends
but people who hated him, mocked him
to the bitter end. Their behaviors they will have
to defend.

Soul

There it is.
Waiting, for freedom
waiting, for queen
waiting, to be seen
what's wrapped around the lonely
Soul ?
Rope? No. Chain ? No.
It's love ready to invade
a heart and fill it
full of warmth that
The sun, can not
Provide.

Dance and poetry

In poetry we use,
periods, comas ,
question marks, and
exclamation points!

In dance they use
the kick, the twirl, the step,
the jump, and a tune. That
too makes an audience swoon.

In poetry we leave our hearts on a sleeve
to expose what we need you to believe .
In dance it's a hand gesture a standing pose.
A costume to let us know she's a rose. As
You can see . Dance and poetry are two
forms of, prose .

The Lonely Snow Tire

The lonely tire swing.
  Hanging on a tree.
  No children to talk to.
  The only time it moves,
  is when the wind blows.
  Is it's emotions feeling. low?
  If   it could talk, what would it say?
  Talk about the children, and dogs, that use to play,
but my friends when its alone.
  Though it has a whole.
  It feels like a cold ancient stone.

Thunder! And Lightening.!

Alone in my home, the sky dark and black
turning day time. into night.
Bolts , of lightning flying a cross the sky ,like a
whip,
Crashing, through the air, making a terrible sound.
They say its just electricity.
This Maybe true for us ,educated few.
But there were times, before we knew.
The Gods were showing us
that we were being disrespectful .
the rumbling, shaking my house,
making me feel like a scared little mouse.

Love .

Love, is up.
Love, is down
Love, is a sound.
Love, is free.
Love, is bound.
Love, is a cloud.
Love, is a sun.
Love.
Love.
Love.
Love is a star.
Love is holding hands.
Love has no demands.

The Witches night.

Cool dark October night.
She and her sisters dance around
The flames, that get higher.
Orange, yellow, and Gold.
Young and old.
Dance.
Dance, hands high in the night sky.
Their voices cries out for the love of
I. Oh my. one by one in order to beat
the sun. They take to their brooms.
Like a mighty wind.
They count to Ten.
They arrive in their Masters, room.

Fall Day

Green, yellow, brown.
The light wind and chirping birds,
  neighborhoods only sound. What a precious
gift from God to be found. he's way of saying.
Lets be clear.
I'm here.

A Leaf

Do we think much of a leaf?
Accept when it's on its tree.
During the summer, providing us with shade.
We feel we have it made.
We love the colors of fall.
With its red, its browns, its yellows
  and oranges. We ooh and ah
them. For a little while.
But once they hit the ground with out a sound.
The leaves we once admired and loved become a
hated yearly, chore.

When Doves Coo.

When my doves coo.
They say hello.
When my doves coo, they
say feed me daddy.
When my doves coo
they Say we love you.
I coo back and say I love
you too .

Kitty laying in the sun.

  He finds,
the light comforts him
it gives him energy.
It gives him security.
He craves the light,
not for sight.
He knows he's being hugged by
God.

love

A look .A touch,
Feeling. Strange body
Reaction. Love is a act
Of mental and physical
Connections.

The plastic bag

Blowing up and down in the wind.
Like a top goes round and round.
Like a ballerina it moves up and down
The wind its only music. When the
Plastic bag blows straight
It moves so fast.   Where is it going?
Barely slowing.   To an unknown
destination.
Why so fast. Are you late?
But when the wind slows and stops.
His journey ends.   But in a recycle bin.
It starts all over again.

Life

Life, is neither light.
Life, is neither dark.
Life, is just life.
Just enjoy your breath,
excite in your heart beat
laugh with love.
Practice a smile.
The rewards will be worth
While.

Sex

A feather on a breast.
A peck on your chest.
On the ear a ,breath.
Touch.
Touch.
Smell.
Smell.
The scent of her soul.
Connections.

The rose bush

A rose bush is like an evil, beautiful, woman.
It sucks you in with its beautiful smells
The delightful colors. Brilliant,
You get in close.
This rose, watch where you grab.
But before you know it.
You been stabbed.

Easter Day

Early, in the morning, one hour of Mass.
The day we celebrate the resurrection.
Noon, arrives too soon.
All of us in our Sunday best.
Not a single minute of rest.
Children, gathering in the back yard.
Finding eggs.   With chocolate candies ,
Jelly beans. Of all colors. And tastes.
In heaven Jesus is looking down.
Smiling at all the celebratory sounds

My African Queen

Hail to my Queen.
Most beautiful woman I have ever seen.
Her body looks like a well carved
Statue.   Her hair is warmth.   When I
Imagine it on my skin.
I imagine it to be the finest silk.
Go, go, she never ever, slows,
Looking into eyes.
I wonder, why?
What does she hide?
To me it doesn't matter.
To me , love   and   joy ,
She only gathers.
She's very active.
Changes lives, saves lives.
I only wish.
If I could. Even if I'm not her Man .
Change and help hers.

Time is:

Time is fast.
Time never last.
It's always in the past.
Time will never be the way we demand.
Time is a cliche.
Time, no matter what we say.
Is never coming when we demand it.
Time is on its on time delay.
No matter how hard we pray.
Time isn't on our display.

Soul Searcher

When a soul searches for a companion,
it uses our flesh as a vessel for its journey.
Looking for   an eternal companion.
Needing touch, needing connection .
Needing those things,   that can turn a small ball
of light,
into the Sun.

Connection

A connection is not just a physical thing.
Its two energies, merging as one. Like the
sun and moon
circling the Earth . Functioning as one to benefit
life.
Keeping each other from
an emotional grave.

Ode to Allergies.

Rotten, Allergies.
Every spring they over come me.
Screwing up my morning.
Nose ever running.   Snot dripping,
dripping,
  down,
  down,
Like a dripping faucet. Eyes itchy.
  My emotions,
making me feel bitchy. Head hurts.
  Hard to breath.
For Canada or Alaska I shall leave. Pollen
I know your needed.   My cherry tree
needs you.
My veggies need you. But, if not for you.
I feel like I got a terrible flue. As a Christian,
I'm not suppose to say this but Allergies , Fuck!
You!

Paranoid ,weather people.

Take cover! Take Cover!
In coming!   Why should
I care?   Why should I dare?
Granted, there can be danger.
However, this is the Midwest.
We know what to do.
Yes it is true.
Don't be scared. Don't be blue.
There's little we can do..
Go in your basement and cower.
This seems to happen every year.
Let's be clear.   They happen, every year.
  Weather men acting like combat reporters.
They stand in rain hitting them in the face.
Mother nature saying, " What are you doing here?"
The storm water hitting the intern in the face.
Like an criminal being sprayed by a can of mace.
Just relax. Its just mother nature wielding her
Ax.   Relax and enjoy the show.
What an exciting way to go!

Cloudy days suck.

Cloudy days suck.
Inside the house. My
Inner mind running
A muck.
Looking forward to the sun.
The warmth beating down on me .
Giving me tons of physical and mental
Energy.
Cloudy days Suck.
The chill in the air.
"Hey this is mid April!   I say
No fair."   "Hey, cloudy days. Why do
You have to so chilly?"
Goose pimples all over my skin.
The strange madness begins.
In may the hours grow longer.
The allergies grow ever stronger.
Then the sneezing then the whizzing. Now that
I think about it. Cloudy, and rainy days.   Don't
suck,
After all.

Allergies

We sneeze, we cough, our eyes itch.
Allergies can be a bitch.
My trash can is a pile of tissue.
It's really becoming an issue.
Sneeze
Sneeze!
SNEEZE!
It's all I do.
My Nose.
RUNS!
Runs!
Runs!!!!!!!!!!
Allergies are no
 Fun.

Everything, can kill   you !

Every day on the news.
The reporter tells me:
Cigarettes can kill me.
Soda pop can kill me.
What can I say.   I hear this,
Every single day.
Even the sports I like to play.
Baseball, football, wrestling,
NASCAR.   Pool, bowling.
What do I do?   What can I say?
My dog can kill me.   My cat can kill me.
My laptop can kill me.
Jesus can kill me.
My sinus pill
Can kill me.
Bubble wrap,
Cooking oil,
Working in toil.
Aluminum foil. Even   the
Soil! Yes, it's true.
Everything! I mean everything
Can kill you.
Guess What!?
Who cares!

A moment in the sun

On a sunny, summers day.
The local boys are on the diamond to play.
Hot Summer's sun beating them down. Even with
a
large crowd, there is not a sound. a man on second
and a man on third. The only noise is a bird.
The home town batter blocks out everything.
Just he and the pitcher. Like a young Jedi he hears
his inner coach say
on this very important day.
" Be the ball . and use the force." in a running
mantra.
" Yes!" he says to himself ,fast ball." With one
mighty
swing a very solid, ding. base hit. a yell every one
watches it fly
all you can say is , Bye, Bye, Bye! a home run a
true moment in the sun
even though its only on Xbox one.

www.ingramcontent.com/pod-product-compliance
Lightning Source LLC
Chambersburg PA
CBHW070247290526
45789CB00004B/1805